ESCHATOLOGIES

ESCHATOLOGIES

John Kinsella

FREMANTLE ARTS CENTRE PRESS

First published 1991 by
FREMANTLE ARTS CENTRE PRESS
193 South Terrace (PO Box 320), South Fremantle
Western Australia, 6162.

Consultant Editor Wendy Jenkins.
Designed by John Douglass.
Production Manager Helen Idle.

Typeset in 11/12 pt Times Roman by City Typesetters, Perth,
and printed on 90 gsm Offset by Lamb Print,
Perth, Western Australia.

National Library of Australia
Cataloguing-in-publication data

Kinsella, John, 1963-
Eschatologies.

ISBN 1 86368 003 9.

I. Title.

A821.3

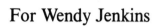

For Wendy Jenkins

Acknowledgements

Poems in this collection have previously appeared in the following publications: *Age, Antipodes, The Australian, Canberra Times, Fineline, Fremantle Arts Review, Imago, Island, LinQ, Otis Rush, Outrider, Overland, Sydney Morning Herald, West Australian, Westerly,* and have been broadcast on ABC and 100 FM radio.

This publication is assisted by the Australia Council, the Australian Government's arts funding and advisory body.

Fremantle Arts Centre Press receives financial assistance from the Western Australian Department for the Arts.

CONTENTS

The Millenarian's Dream

Inland

Inland: storm tides,
ghosts of a sheep weather
alert, the roads uncertain

families cutting the outback
gravel on Sunday mornings,
the old man plying the same track
to and from the session
those afternoons, evenings
(McHenry skidded into a thickset
mallee after a few too many
and was forced to sell up)

On the cusp of summer
an uncertain breeze
rises in grey wisps
over the stubble —
the days are ashen,
moods susceptible,
though it does not take
long to get back
into the swing of things

We take the only highroad
for miles as the centre
of the primum mobile — it's
the eye of the needle
through which our lives'
itineraries must be drawn,
a kind of stone theodolite
measuring our depths beyond
the straight and narrow,
it's a place of borrowed dreams
where the marks of the spirit
have been erased by dust —
the restless topsoil

Burnt Offerings

i past

We thought the whole town had gone up.
From the latticed balcony, the wormy woodwork
creaked as we leaned out further
trying to plumb the tangerine depths.
We caught only the moths flickering
on the edge of the burnt darkness.
                              Apparently,
somebody had pushed an armchair into an open fire.
Only one house had fallen to flame,
the rest to water.

ii present

They say to go down early
if you want the best pickings,
the really dry wood. It's been
heaped up for months now,
though the wet has got into
it a bit — a furlike growth,
white on black skin, taking
over.
        And they say —
                        'If you're
into pyrotechnics, hang around, bring
a few beers down and watch while we pour
kero and petrol over the piles, the flameburst
sucking the air dry, throwing
rat and rabbit fireballs
in all directions . . .'

Rain-gauges

A triptych of rain-gauges
poised over a bore running
ten thousand of salt a day,
as dry as the lips of a pump
idle but for madness, pvc
pipes sweating though unable
to measure their ossification,
and time as brittle as the rings
of a smoked moon marking auras
like triumphs over the Dry & Damned,
the Wanderers, Measurers, Seekers
of Liquid, and those counting
the days since that Spring
morning when the decision
to settle had been taken.

Old Hands/New Tricks

A ring-necked parrot drops into flight,
fence posts collapse and ossify,
the wattle bird trims the lamp of wattle bloom

Despite storm weather the soaks diminish,
though by way of contrast the green tinge
of a late rain pokes its head over stubble —
the new growth that will yield no seed

About the homestead unripe fruit is severed
from trees — parrots jostle, making
swings and see-saws of their bodies

The wells are covered with railway sleepers
over-run with wire-weed and Mediterranean
Bugloss — Salvation Jane — which crisps over
cracks, gives cool water a taste of irony

In the pepper trees magpies threaten to unpick
the world as they know it — their songs are not
characteristic — old hands have learnt new tricks

Two Days Before Harvest

An easterly stretches and compresses
the deadwood fissures, strings of parakeets
arrange themselves into nets to drag
the breeze — their feathers firing,
the sun striking the afternoon pink.

In the soon-to-be lopped heads of wheat
there burns the fidelity of summer — beyond,
on the white-bake of salt, lines of supply
are thinning and the dust of scuffed patches
drinks the blood of eucalypts. Topknot pigeons
encounter themselves, much to their surprise,
in foray from she-oak to powerline and back again.

The tines of a discarded scarifier have set
like the roots of trees ringbarked from memory —
you see, the tractor's welter, the jiggering
blades of the header, the crows teasing
the gate-posts, unlock a continuity
that would persist, or threaten to . . .

The Compression of Time, Place and Incident

Fixed firmly, this comes as landfill,
a sealing of a tomb, a carving
of an epitaph. Too many times
I have sought the first notes
of a tune, the words of a song,
that would break the charm
that's held me to the farmer's words —
'Eagle, I'd remake you if I could.'
   At Wind's Crossing and Eagle Point,
tethered to that ghost known locally
as Hathaways, the farmer stirs
his ti-tree fires and casts iron
loops about the hoop of a wheel,
marks time with a bronze quill,
explores the sound lapse,
insists that somewhere the eagle
is trying to call — landlocked —
unable to reach its eyrie perched
high overhead on the outstretched
arm of a charred York gum,
at the centre of Achille's shield.

Spontaneous Regeneration

I am here to rekindle
the moon dying in its race
for the sun, to break
the puff and bubble of salt,
to entertain the legions
of black-winged stilts
in their long march
to the dam, to harness
the wind dusting
knucklebones of a frayed
and peeling earth, to enter
the season of spontaneous
regeneration
              in company.

Foxes and Python

A fox skin
in a nitrate bath,
and a fox skin drying
stiff as a card
folded over the levers
of a veteran plough,
stare fixedly at a python
coiled about the lintel
of the sheep shed — 'comes
down about once a month
for a feed', the farmer says,
pleased that it remains,
having appeared, like the foxes,
'out of the blue one day'.

Three-in-One Parable

The old fox looks into
the sky which is wider here
than anywhere, while the hunters
sing with their fox whistles
the Song of Asking.

During the day warm spots
settle in the fold of hill,
at night cold winds funnel
deep into the dreams of sheep.

Wells

i

The wire takes hold and spins in the hands,
severing shirt buttons. They pierce the dry
surface and tap clean water ten metres down,
the stigmata of the rough edges brought
through faith in an old timer's electricity.
Or maybe success is merely an aspect of faith,
that if the diviner is a brother or uncle
then you've got to believe in him. Waterwitching
slakes a thirst, greens the garden in places
where Summer forbids this abomination. Though
prayers of affirmation are required to keep
the water flowing — the Underworld has its
limitations and will bleed to death eventually.

ii

Funnelling down to the source —
with a deep well a canvas fly directs
clean air to the digging — then angling
dry stone walls or timbering with jamb posts.
The windlass moves the buckets up and down
simultaneously, meeting somewhere near
centre, though feigning balance. Working
the soft earth you'd wonder how water
could flow anywhere, though hitting rock
you'd wonder how it could ever change its course.
Looking up, the fly is full-blown with light,
the edges of the well are dark lines. The eyes
find it hard to adjust. Sometimes you remember
things like this when the well turns salt.

iii

When the water turns salt, changes course,
or evaporates, they fill the hole with rubbish
from the house, paddocks, and sheds. Cavities
will usually form, making it a dangerous place
to explore. Edges crumble, cave-ins are common,
most often it is fenced off. Sometimes in
the search for a new source, the diviner will
track the ghost of water through its old course
and come to the plugged-up well. Refusing
to believe it possible, though unable to curb
their curiosity, more often than not farmers will
have the old well tested. The look on their faces
when they are told the water is clean and plentiful!

When I Go Alone

i

When I go alone
through the trill of stubble
into the salt
I do so
not in the moment
but in memory surveyed and chartered
in some softer place.

Saltweed
ropes at my ankles,
erosion
channels my feet
and breaks each particle
away from its platform —
a flight of mountain ducks
erupts from the dam.

ii

A modicum of Self
will outgrow its best intention — the magpies swagger
and are full of mourning, would seem to gloat,
would tear intruders apart, it is not their end
on which they're brooding: this is nesting season.

iii

In the gnarled gullies
of Two People's Bay
the noisy scrub bird
builds its song
to the point of bursting,
not for human ears
it will cut the skin of the drum,
a sharp sound made empty.

I have skirted its territory as a child
unwittingly,
a cousin has tracked its song,
though none I know
has seen it / it has been said
        that on rare occasions
           it will mimic
        a human call for help,
           of joy.

iv

At canopy level
crossing a swing bridge
that floats on tension
I note the crumbling banks
the diminishing river
and catch the sensual patter
of thinning water, a voyeur
with a squint . . .

V

When I go alone
I accept that only animals
have souls and I must
court their blessings.

The magic
is in the naming —
though who's to trust
these guides and dictionaries?
Surely the name a creature
gives itself is spoken privately —
amongst its kindred, at a territorial
meeting, before setting out
on a migratory passage?

Maybe
all Namings are imminent —
that all shall be said
in the moment intervention
is accepted.

The Myth of the Grave

i

A pair of painted quails
scurries across the quills of stubble
a flurry of rapid
eye movement

they shadow my walk
ostentatiously
lifting and dropping
into invisible alleyways

reaching the grave
I turn to catch them
curving back, stopped
by the windrows

the grave is a magnet
that switches polarity
when you reach it.

ii

The epitaph is measured
by the size of the plaque,
or is it the plaque that's
measured by the epitaph?

It seems to matter.
Death becomes a question
of economy — the lavish are big
on ceremony, slight on prayer.

iii

At a distance
sheep leave salt-licks
beside a dam and zig-zag
down towards the shade.

Grey gums bend with the tide
of the breeze, the midday sun
would carry their doubles
to the grave and fill the urns.

The ground dries and crumbles,
a lizard darts out of a crack
and races across the paddock.
Do ashes rest easily here?

iv

A fresh grave that holds three
generations is something you question
on a first encounter. How in life
would they have felt about sharing

a single room in a shoebox flat?
Maybe, at an instant, only one soul
is resident, the others entering the bodies
of quails, exploring the wastes of stubble.

Voices From a Region
of Extraction

Miner

Old Tin Lizzie
was the first car
in Kookynie — the fella
owed me money and wanted me
to take it in payment,
the kids pestering
and me understanding
that most of all they wanted
to be the first kids in town,
for a little while at least.

I told them we couldn't
afford to run it . . .

Miner's Wife

From Perth to Woorooloo
the train wheezed and rasped,
clanked and jostled.

The sanitorium opened
on one side to allow
fresh air, protected
by no more than blinds
during storm weather,
which the men who couldn't
garden contemplated
opening and closing.

The chill morning air
would bite like razors
into their collapsing chests.
This was the open-air treatment.

The children, arms laden
with flowers grown in rich soil,
played at their feet,
and they harboured no bitterness.

Miner

Despite a dozen hotels
I would continue past all, straight
to the coffee palace with its wood
and whitewashed hessian walls.

I was happiest when working the Cosmopolitan,
it being in the middle of the town
and not much travelling.

And the war stripped the district
clean to the bone,
and the few mines left open
worked frantically.

Miner's Wife

I mean, he had to tell them himself
really, didn't he?

From Woorooloo to Perth
the train clanked and jostled,
wheezed and rasped
in tireless travel . . .

Miner

She tells me the eldest
is working as a seamstress
and can no longer visit
on weekends.

I get them to bring me
the newspapers . . . I read
year after year
of the continuing boom.

They came once, the photographers
from the newspaper — the city newspaper —
and had us all sitting there: bleached, dry,
though liquid faced.

Miner's Wife

And then I caught the boy
floating in the red creek
in an old rainwater tank,
though I left him to it,
it not having rained
for months.

And I said that if my church isn't good enough,
then I'll be damned if I'll go into hers.

And I left water
on the verandah
for the wanderers
of the desert
and respected
the spirits.

Miner

Once lost in the desert
it becomes the fullest memory.

Where those who weary
of their clothes
scream for cover
in the hours before sunrise.

The red desert,
where every particle
howls . . .

Afghans came in the end.
On camels . . . with their clocks,
boxes, and scented furniture.
They gave me water.
The town was almost dry.

Miner's Wife

His lips were blue.
I've barely room for this.
And to find a place for it
in this household of a brain
I've been left with after
years of shuffling our lives.
Ah, his feet so cold
his eyes glazed and receding,
his lips . . . cornflowers.

Pillars of Salt

We always look back,
attracted by that feeling
of having been there before — the roads
sinking, the soil weeping (scab on scab
lifted), fences sunk to gullies
catching the garbage of paddocks,
strainers blocked by stubble
and machinery and the rungs
of collapsed rainwater tanks / and maybe
the chimney and fireplace
of a corroded farmhouse, once
the guts of the storm, now
a salty trinket.

The salt is a frozen waste
in a place too hot for its own good,
it is the burnt-out core of earth's eye,
the excess of white blood cells.
The ball-and-chain rides lushly
over its polishing surface, even dead wood
whittles itself out of the picture.

Salt crunches like sugar-glass, the sheets
lifting on the soles of shoes (thongs scatter
pieces beyond the hope of repair) — finches
and flies quibble on the thick fingers
of salt bushes, a dugite spits
blood into the brine.

An airforce trainer jet appears,
the mantis pilot — dark eyed and wire
jawed — sets sight on the white wastes
for a strafing run: diving, pulling out
abruptly, refusing to consummate.
                              Salt
explodes silently, with the animation
of an inorganic life, a sheep's skull no more
than its signature, refugees already
climbing towards the sun
on pillars of salt.

The Millenarian's Dream

i

On the Glad Day the sheep
penned themselves and offered
their wool willingly.
An old shearer was seen standing
on an outcrop of quartz down
by the 'thousand acre' paddock.
At the pub that night somebody
said he'd been on fire. The old
shearer denied it, saying
it must have been the sunset.

ii

The sky's props popped and crackled
as they struggled to hold their burden,
even ghosts moved en-masse out of the mulga
to witness what promised to be a holocaust.

iii

The five-pointed flower
struggled to outgrow
                        outshine
the darkest polypus: the spent tin mine
they'd blocked with a few sticks
of gelignite after a couple of kids
had fallen in and perished

the crows spreading
as the heat peeled
the layers of sight.

iv

Intaglioed on the silo walls
the cat and its litter inflected
the bloodier face of wheat: ASW,
Australian Standard White.

They hooted and cheered
in the pub that night, washing
it down straight from the tap,
while in the limelight

a stranger had sat, marking
dust and twisting a glass,
clenching a fist, wiping
rust from his lips.

v

These are only a few of the many images
that came to mind as cosmonauts 999 Days
and 1000 Days watched Mother Earth shade
herself like a child's etcho-sketch.

The sun, caught in the child's decline
refused to rise, while the larks
fired between the cosmonauts' eyes,
outspun the concentric layers of sight.

Counterfeit

Lasseter
knew the will-o-the-wisp
to be no more
than freedom's counterfeit

from the heart
of conflagration
he knew

from the core
of reef
he knew

and the will-o-the-wisp
loved him for this.

Photism

It wasn't gold
but girasol

And though beautiful
in its own right

Perceptual and spilling fire
the miners unsettled

The bones of Lasseter,
ground the spirits

Of the place to dust
and squeezed tight

The earthplates.
Need it be said

The girasol wept
tears of blood.

The Shedding

The mulga ghost
skirts its thinning shores

Sings its impenetrable centre —
richer than this atmosphere

Of gold dust and a bloodshot iris.
Light-footed under heavy skies

It barely activates Daniel's
second half — cryptaesthesia

A slow-moving bird whose territory
stretches no further than the tomb

Of reef, a grey or even green blur
on the frame of the photograph.

Every boom or bust story
has its boundaries, and even

Prophets fail to predict the precise
time of a shedding.

Catchment

Catchment

i   zone

In a catchment zone the keepers
must keep clean houses, sweeping
soot from the roots, scouring
granite outcrops regularly.

The catchment's focus — a saline pool,
comfortable in its illusion of deep, clear water —
sheds itself in the stubs of severed trees
hedging the waterline.

ii   quarry

Examining the dross of a quarry,
(the coarse and fine sizes), we may grasp
what it is that has reduced things to this:

the panorama sliced away in cross section,
exposing the roots in their bed of rock;
or in the deeper layers, the mechanism driving
the rust of ironface, feeding the surface's scrub,
slipped buttresses, cliff faces . . .
                        the risk of overextension
threatening the pristine catchment:
the quarry top seeking to cover the wounds.

iii   pipes and valves

We scale the wall, rising up over the filaments
of pumping station — pipes, straitjacketed,
annelids splitting and regenerating in and out
of the slinking earth, skirting the valley,
entwining undergrowth

                          the valves feeding
from their concrete outriggers (weir-houses
inhabited by pressure gauges, clacks, and screws),
their task reason enough for existence, thoughts
on source and destination not one of their strongpoints.

iv   the wider waters

Sloughs of mosquitoes squeezing in and out
of sluices in a hillside cast barely
a collective shadow over the catchment.

At the foot of a spillway, past seasons
wallow in brackish puddles, raft insects
eke out sketchy existences
                         thin lines of pines
cling to retainer walls.

From the summit — the barrier neither moulded nor bound
by roots, but soldered to the squared shoulders
of valley — we look to the liquid centre: wind slicks
flattening the ripples, ironing them out, wiping
the corrugated glass clean, darning patches
on the wider waters.

At the Serpentine Pipehead

Defrocked camellias,
their discarded skirts
rotting in unceremonious heaps —
*The Water Board hopes you have
enjoyed your visit, welcomes
suggestions* — I suggest the plum flower,
the almond blossom . . . I suggest the song
of a lorikeet cast like a net
through the deadwood of spent trees,
I suggest the area closed off
because of dangerous chemicals,
I suggest the solitary catboat,
its limp sail a premonition,
a marooned pilotless ferry
on the distant bank.

Crossing the wall of the small pipehead
a child crouches to view the waters,
through the space between fence
and concrete — the green mesh confusing
the picture, preventing pure vision.
I trace the lime-sweat tributaries:
spread like bruised capillaries
they broach the hairline cracks of the walkway.
I admire the lichen welding the walls:
no talus-creep, these rocks have fallen neatly
into place, though the position of hills
and filtered river is by chance.

Metaxu

i Patterson's Curse/Salvation Jane

It's what you do when the chips are down,
or when transport and a few hours
present themselves — passing the overflow
of Patterson's Curse   (spillage riding the firebreaks
                       deep down the slopes, sloshing
                       at the walls of the saddle dam,
                       double sown at the edge of road,
                       embroidered by stock . . .)
                                        The wattle & daub
of the catchment's absorbent surface — the jarrah
and bracken ferns, wildflowers and lemon-scented gums
(with blackened bases like the termite-free power poles
of suburban streets), the magnified credulity
of a patch of skin.
                 Internal vibration to compact cement —
though, as usual, I place my hands to sense the warmth
that movement brings and find none greater
than that reflected from the spread of curiosity.
                                  Unseen,
the tunnel forms the true bridge, though it's hard
to come to grips with this when you're sailing the perfect
course of the wall: between water and air, blue sky
and dark rock, heavy clouds and a glimpse of a would-be
phosphorescence in the heart of the waters.
                          Though the tunnel
carries more than implications of a saturated life:
                              granite
& dolerite dykes rock-bolted, slabbed to the floor of a vast
building that has as its roof the floor of the catchment;
and maybe the core of that purple encroachment —
                            Salvation Jane.

ii Filters

Filters — you set them up to prevent the truth
with its rough-hewn aggregate crushing you down
and damming the flood — you quote purity — maybe
silently, but letting it creep into gestures,
a lack of patience — you can feel the tension
in the wall. As you sit on a granite outcrop
looking up at the dark face, an aspect of seepage
(from the galleries your scream of 'Watch out!
It's going to burst!' can only be heard by
other inspectors) will traverse the interlock
of tightened space as easily as rain shatters
the prospect of a leisurely walk through
the catchment (Jarrah Dieback — you are near
a Forest Disease Risk Area: Quarantine   Horse
or Vehicle is Prohibited) and sickness is a monolith
movable only by sound mechanics.
                            Leakage paths are woven
by frogs, the flight paths of crow and cockatoo,
the crack and regurgitation of warblers, the bantering
of 28s . . . They mark time, we count our steps back
to transport, we do not risk holding hands, an embrace —
we are treading water, the taps carry rust
preserved in the wall-crack, history turned
in the crusher barrels, the size greater than its gauge,
the tension no longer filtered . . . our love percolates,
is filtered in its own making, is the seepage
that defies the walls, attempts to bridge the gap.

Stretching the Vista

A strelitzia parts the folds
of humidity with its beak
of cartilage — but don't be fooled,
it's just held out against
the year's last frosts,
and its foliage flexes confidence.
The risk here is to be channelled
into a particular vista, that caught
in the concrete spillway
you may fail to realise
that a bird of paradise
will fly unnoticed in this unfamiliar
territory — where blue-green water
spreads wide to its sienna rim,
makes islands and bottlenecks
of land look luxuriant.
Stretching the vista in all directions
a bearded dragon zig-zags
over the dam's drier face,
a clockwork ziggurat restrains
a tense silence — white horses
warm to a desert wind and swim
against the anchored points
of a tourist compass. The lack
of overflow teases the laden clouds
without making them spill their hearts,
the wind continues its seduction
in playing the jarrah strings
of the catchment lyre,
the pink flute of erosion.

Pipeline

The pipeline cleaves the catchment
with its good intention — on a watersling
outflowing the silver jacket, palmed
off by pumping station after pumping
station, though losing none of its spring,
darting forwards with a hop, skip, and a jump,
riding sidecar to a national highway,
swinging from one climate to another
without a change of expression.
                                                    An egret flies
lower over a coastal reservoir, parrots
in unclaimed territory know the pipeline
to be a hot cable that will burn through claw,
a crow senses moisture at the final
pumping station.
                              In passing, it remains
indifferent to farm machinery, to the crisp
and wink of saltpans, to finches tossing
their hoods back and tittering
about its stiff shell.
                              In passing, it gloats inwardly
before leaving a dry wind that's been shooting
its skin to wrestle with scrub, before plunging
headfirst into red earth.

Victoria Dam

Crossing the spillway, contrary
to the line of flow, casting
back over the dross, slicing
banks, drainage, liquid
tailings, you find the shoulder —
dam wall curving away,
like a rock on a string,
car accelerating into a corner,
tension dragging it in.

The sun sinks into the socket
of valley, an eye nerved
with green blood of canopy
covering the escape
or evacuation of fresh and stale
water mingled. Powerlines coaxing
overhead, though indifferent
to the mud up to your ankles.

Escorted and then abandoned
to the mechanics of the poem,
you cable echoes, ringing
out of the damp basin on
tenuous rungs of shadow.
White-trunked sentinels
stare bemused — so, this
is what's at the bottom of it!

The rough and the smooth
face of the spillway wall — the dry
as smooth as glass, the wet
rough, lime-leached, disconsolate,
despite its extra skin (blood
had crept up and sourced new veins).

            The basin flicks
the wind up as you stand on the lip
of spillway, sifting a birdcall
unrecognised. Below, scabs form
over an emptied heart, a desert
walled by forest.

Vehicles congest on the far abutment —
like a wake they laugh, come maybe
for the felling, breath spent,
marking out their takings. You notice
prints of track-driven machinery
set in cement near the base of wall.
An engineer considers the dam —
'Water leaching through the wall
has sucked lime out of the matrix —
the concrete is crumbling,
the iron inside is rusting
and an explosion is possible,
even a tremor could set
the whole thing off'. Ti-tree
has lanced its roots deep, clutching
aggregate, distorting flow tests.

From White Gates up to Old Victoria,
then to tanks in Kalamunda, Lesmurdie,
Wallaston, and Bickley, water swinging
its way up and out of the catchment.
The ranger sings, 'It's the rhythm
you want, the rhythm of White Gates
and Old Victoria'. He says the cement
that holds the walls was shipped by clipper
from England, that if it was left
another year it would reach a hundred.
Though he has to admit, you could take
a shower by standing beneath the leaks.

In the half-light an engineer
takes stock and sight of the white-boxed
seismic recorder, climate station,
survey pillars — he wanders towards
the marker flags, forerunners
of the new dam. 'Dam engineers
talk of downstream, drainage
engineers talk upstream', he laughs.
His arms arc through forest.
When the old dam was drained
birds came in waves and picked
reef on reef of freshwater mussels
left stranded. Siphoned,
the flesh-centred aggregate
bleeds as the moon dominates,
as we make our way up or down stream.

Retired Reservoir

A cleft between hills stripped
to gravel and black granite, brief
stands of jarrah and gums heavily scarred,
a thin wall etched with seepage's motif.

I stand on high ground and glance
down onto the wall, its rocky shoulder
soothed by overflow, the comfort of white water,
an unseen creek below gathering confidence.

Rain cuts up through the valley
and thuds against the pitted face,
which disappears, cut off by the testimony
of birdcall. Clouds clot on a precipice.

I cannot take the many paths towards
the valley's centre — their surfaces
are temporary, while mere thought erodes,
and birdcall cuts water's salient devices.

Plumburst

The Orchardist

Orange trees cling
to the tin walls
of his home. A red
checked shirt and grey
pair of trousers hang
over the one-eyed tractor.
His oranges are small suns
and he is an astronaut
floating slowly
through their spheres
of influence.

The Orchard

1

It is not my place, though he seeks
to make it this. Overcome by the city
it is in need of defence. I think he would like
a gang of strong arms to protect against the gangs
of his delusions, to ward off the organised,
the planned attrition. I offer words, and in hard times
these are almost enough. I speak to truants,
warning them off, apologising for a scared
old man threatening with his pitchfork.

2

Seen from the heart of the picking — astride
the gridwork of trees — the vacancies are voids
through which predators and visitors will plot
their course. In itself, this is as it should be,
but something doesn't fit into the picture
of 'paths coincident on being anon twin halves
of one august event', or maybe this is a puzzle
of material, labour, and event, from which some vital
piece is missing, or has been overlooked.

A Field of White Butterflies

There is a lot of mystery in me . . .
he explains, peering deep into my eyes.
As a child I would examine the smallest
things, things that would not ordinarily
be seen. My mother would tell the neighbours
that I was a daydreamer, there was no other way
of explaining it. That was in a very
cold place, high in the mountains
above Dalmatia in Yugoslavia.
I came here when I was eighteen
looking for work. I knew about
the languages of animals and plants.

Three seasons ago you couldn't
look at this paddock without seeing
a white butterfly — consuming, crowding
even themselves out of existence.
Last season I saw two, two white butterflies
in the whole year. This year the Monarch
will come, mark my words — wandering
down over the hills, settling
pince-nez on the potato flowers.
You see, where people settle
imbalance follows, the air
being full of white butterflies,
or there being no white butterflies at all.

Ibis

An ibis picks between thin veins
of grass surfacing on open ground,
recently upturned, nourished in mist
and exhumed by the morning sun.

Stilt-legged it stalks on a pivot,
graceful in its geometrics.
It is difficult to pinpoint
the centre of balance,
which imparts a life of its own.

In flight it lunges slowly
as though it were not meant
to be airborne, its legs
tight outriggers, mouthpiece
a curved pipette
drawing and discharging
the grey-blue sky.

I also remain afloat
— an ibis — riding the crests
and troughs of a changing surface,
settling on aspects of thought,
treading lightly the outskirts.

Ibis Myth

Ibises fan out over
a paddock next to an arterial road
welling under the residue of rains,
and work their black beaks
systematically. We move with them.
Should the scene be brightened
by ignoring the houses, powerlines,
fuel leaking from a petrol station?
Ibises are precise in their scansion.
Not a brief glimpse, we must consider,
that interpretation comes later — the image
consumes the sullen plains, the flock
will fly (in Grace). Stretching
from centre to extremity,
the myth accounts
for the adaptable . . . the one straw-necked ibis
                       moves freely with nine
                       of the sacred variety.

On Albert Tucker's *Ibis In Swamp*

What action prevails
in the miasma of swamp?
The mummified ibis reflects/reflected
in the crescent of its black moon beak.
Life almost crisp amongst decay
makes decay necessary

                        even muted flowers

become profoundly
beautiful.

Sacred Ibis wades green light
thick with shadows, the stilled eye
accepts the dark heart welling
in its hollowed log.

The Essence of Camellias

The essence of created things
is to be intermediaries.

Simone Weil

Past their moment
Citizens
      of a bruised empire
  an imperial red
          crushed under,
That not even
      the naivety
Of a Rousseau
      could capture.
Beneath the glossed sun
          of memory
Rosettes vitrify,
      their essence
Mimicking
    the created shape.

Camellias, prima donnas
      of the pyrotechnic,
Their dance floor
      humus black.

Paperbarks

Paperbarks scream out of childhood
deep into wetlands — lightning, a silver flash
of the fringe, though as subliminal as ghosts,
their territory that of the spirit.
Water fallen, dank goitres tease
our thirst, skins peel and flake
about the grasping roots, sweltering
in the red tinge of earth. Though holding light
absorbent skins will not extinguish when voice
falls and memory lingers, for these are ghosts
who sing the stagnant weathers,
and brew storms out of drought.

The Bottlebrush Flowers

A Council-approved replacement
for box trees along the verges
of suburban roads, it embarrasses
with its too sudden blush — stunning
at first, then a burning reminder
of something you'd rather forget.
And it unclothes so ungraciously —
its semi-clad, mangy, slovenly,
first-thing-in-the-morning appearance.
And while I've heard it called
a bristling firelick, a spiral
of Southern Lights, I've also seen
honey-eaters bob upside down
and unpick its light in seconds.

Plumburst

for Wendy

The neat greens of Monument Hill
roll into sea, over the rise the soft rain
of plumfall deceives us in its groundburst.

If lightning strikes from the ground up,
and Heaven is but an irritation that prompts
its angry spark, then plums are born
dishevelled on the ground and rise
towards perfection . . .

Out of the range of rising plums
we mark the territory of the garden,
testing caprock with Judas trees,
pacing out melon runs. Behind us a block
of flats hums into dusk and the sun
bursts a plum mid-flight.

Windows

i

You follow the smoke-column
from a garden fire to a point
near the top of the window
where it liaises with the dark
waste of clouds. From the ash,
still warm, the bulbs — electric —
throw off their shucks.

ii

The wind stirs a vague notion
from its frame — the sweep
of the Sleepy Mallow of Peru,
the shimmering Arizona Cypress,
the hillocked paddocks,
the cankered orchard,
the errant hawk riding the boundaries,
and a fell moon straining to claw
the inhabitants of a dark room
out into the finest of days.

Strange Metaphors

Dry Dock Sculpture

On the mantelpiece
a Giacometti
sits in company
just as is,
holding itself well,
a stretched body
standing up
to the decay
of a damask rose
in miniature vase —
a Giacometti
on the mantelpiece —
an earthbound figurehead,
a vessel without sails.

Kenneth Noland's *A Warm Sound In A Gray Field, 1963*.

A warm sound in a gray field
finds it may break out consistently,
letting the breath of discovery
flow in rings spread warmly
out over a gray field.

The bell chime — love's corona —
feeds back into itself,
through all landscapes,
a variety of atmospheres,
trembling imperceptibly
at the centre.

There is a point where tensions
grip the heart, where darkness
seeks a glimpse; though all is quiet
as a warm sound in a gray field
steps in to play its part.

the insulation of the new york sonnet

for Noel Sheridan

I don't know if there's such a thing
as the new york sonnet, and I can't find
out until I get my copy of Denby back
from a guy who shot through to Carnarvon
at short notice. It's not likely that
tracking stations, bananas, racism, and
the Gascoyne River, are going to yield
a response, but Denby, to whom you handed
a cup of tears some years ago in a film
that was rumoured to be a sonnet in itself,
holds the answer, not so much in the dance
of language, but in his collecting insulators
from the tops of power pylons and giving them
as tokens of gratitude to his closest friends.

Dissolving

Those gods made permanent by photochemistry
rise dripping from the tanks of inky fluids,
rehearsing their tricks of significance —
John Tranter

In the one solution any number of images
will be dissolving simultaneously;
take this short from a soon to be released
video: the dealer moves into a free
transit zone, packing an electric drill
and looking like a powder monkey, the wind
licks the bowl of the river and sings
a ditty that goes something like this — *and*
those who ping speed, whack smack, hit coke,
blat angel dust, cook acid, will taste
anything that gives a rush. The flesh
squabbles about the anode and cathode
of its own solution, while people from
the censorship board note where each
particle travels, how long it takes to disperse
and congregate. Charged by the cut and thrust
of expectation, travelling the frescoed
halls and filling the pink stucco rooms
of the script, you forget that interval
is a small drama in itself — that maybe
the sappers working at the base of the bridge
have a lot to do with the dissolving storyline,
that the zodiac bobbing lightly will take
photographers, sound mixers, seagulls,
and the train passing overhead, out
of the picture before you've had a chance
to get back into the theatre for the second
half, before that drug dealer has dissolved
the drug, filled your electric veins.

Eschatology

Best left unsaid. Reflect the day
the earth stood still. Consider.

You collect partitions. Meteor trains
tubing their cold way through space.

And the desert is the same. Partitions.
Sub-divisions split from the soul.

Too much the cold months on all planets.
Too much.   Fromme's

death cantoes roll on arcanely,
parodying their binding. In desert

the structure of our fortune
can be examined in the sand's snaking,

the vicissitude of starlight,
the realignment of body fluids.

Heaven's flat green fields welding
the globe. Partitioned from space.

Strange Metaphors

'Isn't he the guy who uses strange metaphors — like
describing cars with teeth?'
Anthony Lawrence

Collapse is wild with symmetry
and mechanical savants move with artistic
hands — making poetry out of the angry
expressions of car grills. The drinks
waiter steps in just in the nick of time
and offers a vision of a sturgeon sailing
through flaccid waters driven by an ambient
wind, getting no further than the length
of its entrails. The clean-shaven makes
a cameo appearance, the grey barrel suit
setting the forget-me-not off perfectly.
After all, we are poets, and have got to be
able to make sense of this. Look! Quickly
the wedge-tailed eagle takes leave of its
broken body — no time to waste, it's a long flight
back to the Nullarbor. And, great joy, the day
is ours — watch Ashberry dip into a hint of Rilke
and lodge himself delicately amongst our words.
Though let's be wary and not display the trophy
yet — somebody at a distant table is suggesting
that there's more than a hint of ghost writer
about this, that strange metaphors have been
forced to do their captor's bidding.

The James Dickey Poems

Divining James Dickey

The pages flit about the binding.
Water witching my fingers idle words
on waters of Braille. Chosen
carefully it reads: *Now in the last*
stand of wheat they bend and   as
if to increase the odds   *For under*
the mild white sun. Stretching.
Ewes with six kilos of wool on their backs
clean their arses on a blowtorch.

Divining brings motive to question.
An in-built acceptance that lumps Fate
on its victims, soothed under the mild
white sun, bending with words tight
to the pasture, enmeshed in wheat.

the music

James Dickey comes back to me
under the Norfolk pine trees —

I am the *sweet flesh* he'd enjoy
hunting, flaying and splaying

as a trophy, a notch on the 3D
screen of poetry, the distillation

of a prayer. You too are of this flesh,
as are the tracks left by a bear

or bison, the droppings of a wild turkey.
James Dickey comes back to me

beneath the Norfolk pine trees,
his blade probing its skin, its hair.

the flawed imperative

The page moves with
the knife blow of the pen,
the zipper of an anorak
clicks slowly, driven against
a cold that would make metal
brittle, seize the mechanism,
no matter how simple.
                              Cold air,
held tight to the chest,
the warmth of two bodies pressed
close together replicated,
our love is always distant,
and absent when forest
closes over — day's end.
                              Take
the mountain path, avoid the lower
ground — you should write this also,
if you can anchor the page
to the scent of animals
turning in their graves, on the surface.
Nearing a road, the outskirts
of a town — timber country,
an axe swings and rings
you to its blow, the iron
meridian bracing flesh
to bones. And thinking — now!

Seize the moment! Take aim
blindly and loose your arrow,
discard the measured step,
the hunter's respect,
rend the ashen lake of dusk.

the moon, a thumbprint with hollowed veins

The moon, a thumbprint with hollowed veins
(marking the shining eye of the page), risks
extinction in courting an old woman's prayers,
for through her all aspirations are focussed,
concentrated; and should she be a poet,
or have had a poet lover in her youth,
the moon's danger would be double-enhanced.
But the moon cannot mark its thoughts indelible
on the jailor's page with a mere hot press
of its thumb, and a wolf at its feet will taste
only the scent of the jailor in its blood,
for its veins are thickly filled, and the hunter's
call (eyes pressed to the moon) marks the steel,
a thumbprint with hollowed veins, the page.

The Vegetable King

Taking the shape
Of the Vegetable King
Leaves little room for enjoying
What's offered to our boney
Hearts; I say, let him in, take
Fluid, skin, and fibre, and bind
Your flowing, let
Sight imbue blood
and shadow.

                The Vegetable King
Sets nets to catch the fragments
Of our bodies, his maleness
A comfort, though careful
Where his hair-roots lead; saturnalia,
A turning of earth in every
Loamy cup that's spent
Ripening his crown or tuber —
And in his gratitude
Taking stock of what could be
If the weather were to turn,
Or his potency fail — reciting
Always, to the mother, the
deus misereatur, growing
With the flow, from heart
To shadow, Heaven to grave.

The Rites of James Dickey

They fall, they are torn,
They rise, they walk again.
'The Heaven Of Animals'

Nothing lost, nothing gained,
Instinct or knowledge blind in pain;
A slow chair rocks on the edge
Of the forest, the herding
Of death and marriage — nuptials
Bright on the covers, lush
With a day's work spent in the wire's
Tension: sunrise suspended, ecstatic
Death rekindled, this the torn flesh
Preparing to rise and settle again.

They fall, they are torn,
They rise, they walk again.

Polishing bones bleached in Heaven,
Returned via the arrow's tip, pre-
Cursor to prescience, spark
As strong as wire, the arrow
A beak furrowing an already green
Surface. The forest unnaturally
Still — storm-waiting, lavishing
Silence on tension. Confused, animals
Walk new climates, localities, their
Habits complying no longer.

They fall, they are torn,
They rise, they walk again.

And sleepers are restless,
The pits of their Unknowing
Filled — light forcing the wound,
Blood nor flesh able to drive
It out. The singer, the maker
Of the sermon, feeling ground
Loosen, air grow thin, sky
Bellowing close to his skin,
His soul moving out towards
The Heaven Of Animals.

fait accompli

Death performs
With the pain of accuracy —
What trees refuse
The flesh of stone
Absorbs — We the dancers
Empty handed,
Electric and fragile
On the tips
Of our toes.

To the tips
Of our fingers
We are expected to dance
The floor of canyons
Sun-white, though
As sharp as frost.
The body cramps,
Celebrations
End. The animal sun,
The animal moon,
Singing the hunter,
His emptied veins,
The music of sinew
and taut muscles,
Of the leap frozen
In sleep.

Parahelion Over Foreshore/By Extension

a red ball is held between the sun and its child,
a red ball is held between the sun and its child . . .

the child looks up and the red ball eclipses its parent,
the child looks up and the red ball eclipses its parent . . .

the sun burns the arm away that holds the red ball
twice over

        the arm gone the ball seems to float
        the arm gone the ball seems to float

twice over
the sun burns the arm away that holds the red ball

the corpses of blowfish strewn on the jetty's deck,
the corpses of blowfish strewn on the jetty's deck
disturb him/by extension . . .
                over the edge the sun smiles
                over the edge the sun smiles
an arm reaches out
an arm reaches out
        holding a red ball
        holding a red ball

the child looks up and the red ball eclipses its parent,
the corpses of blowfish strewn on the jetty's deck
disturb him/by extension . . .
                over the edge the sun smiles
                holding a red ball
                an arm reaches out,
A red ball is held between the sun and its child

mondrian/laboratory/
mounting pedestals

the fume cupboards
that must accompany
stacks on the roof
of a laboratory
infuse the notion
that ibises
were manufactured
as prototype
Concorde airliners/
that Mondrian's *Starry*
Sky above the Sea
is the fracture
of luminosity's eloquence:
when stacks strive
for an art that becomes
the random discharge
of particles mounted
on a pedestal
in a room composed
of form's colourful
building blocks

Still Life/Pavilion and Cherry

HOME   VISITORS
an empty oval
draws sight
to the bare pitch,
with more than a green tinge
it rolls itself flat,
a strip of film

the bowler
breaks the stumps
at the *river end*,
someone had shaped
to glance — blinded
by the sun reflecting
off the freshly painted
pavilion

some time back
a stranger was killed
in the outfield,
a cherry dropping
from the sky,
lost in the swirl
of lights, striking
head-on.

Lilith

For I am the first and the last.
I am the honoured one and the scorned one.
I am the wife and the virgin . . .
I am the barren one,
 and many are her sons . . .
I am the silence that is incomprehensible . . .
I am the utterance of my name.
Thunder, Perfect Mind 13:16-14:15 from The Nag
Hammadi Library, edited by James M. Robinson.

Nightly thy tempting comes, when the dark breeze
scatters my thought among the unquiet trees
and sweeps it, with dead leaves, o'er widow'd lands
and kingdoms conquer'd by no human hands
C.J. Brennan, Poems 1913

The Ribs of Adam

The first Eve failed the adamtest —
how many ribs do I have? he asked.
She could not answer and faded
back into the dirt of Paradise.
The second Eve guessed right,
with a little help from the serpent,
who was not Baal but Lilith
on a Narcissus kick.

Libation

She poured thick red wine
from the cup over her stomach
and ran her fingers through it.
This is a libation for myself
she said, this is my self love
   this is my self hatred
   this is my defeatism
   this is my id floating
on a tide of my own blood,
this is a waste of perfectly
good wine.

A Centurion's Wife

Odd that an extra
member of *his* entourage
should raise her head
after so many years.
That not even the gnostics
had ventured to mention
this hanger-on, malingerer
who'd managed to install
herself in the sacred tomb.

That it was she who gathered
crumbs from under the table,
delivered loaves, consoled
lepers as sores re-opened.
That it was she who sought
life in the tree withered
in its failure to bear fruit,
returned coins, saved
fish from the nets.

The Machinist

I'm probably saying more than I should
when I bring to your mind those five women
in Picasso's *Les Demoiselles d'Avignon* — I am
the one on the top left, though looking a little
less angular now, age and life having rounded
my figure. So, here I am, in this far away
from anywhere country, in old age, mourning
my lostlife. Yes, I do have children, and no
I never married. Actually, my son died
not so long ago. Both daughters are married,
one to an artist whose paintings sell for anything.
Strange that you should come here and ask
about my life . . . has somebody identified me
from that painting? Did Picasso leave notes?

Notes on the Succuba

*the sacred owl shall also rest there, and
find for herself a place of rest*
Isaiah 34:14

Folding her wings
the succuba settles.

In this dream she rides
high above the earth,
refusing the recumbent position,
recycling her love.

*

The Ineffable Name spoken
the nightjar dislodged darkness
made ash of the stars.

The averted face,
the seed that is blood,
the weeping that eats
at her offspring.

*

The city lights
are old childless women
she has left stranded.

When a child laughs
in its sleep
they flick its nose:
a charm against Lilith,
the ring about her neck.

But Lilith loves.
Lilith is the sunflower
tracking the sun.

                    *

the shape of the dance
is the shape of the journey
is the shape of waking
is the shape of conjecture
bursting out of itself

the shape of the music
is the shape of sight
is the shape of taste
is the shape of night
is the shape of the dance   (of life)
lost to its own choreography,
     morphology

                    *

The seduction of dreaming?
How many lie with minds open
lusting after the vision (beautiful),
tempted by their own creation?

And of Senoi, Sansenoi, and Sammangelof:
their rings are her prison.

                         *

the sacred owl
grown restless,
climate and circumstance
changing, sidewinds,
(broken winged)
across the darkening
sand

Lilith Secretes Herself
in the Creation of a
Nietzschean Aphorism

Standing in the garden
Nietzsche bent down, plucked
a flower, and held it to his nose.
In the act of picking this flower
Nietzsche lost track of Necessity,
or Necessity lost track of Nietzsche.
A voice whispered in his ear:
'You have succumbed to desire my dear'.

Lilith on Renaissance Gardens

i   the trophies of marius

From the 1499 edition
of the Hypnerotomachia Poliphili
we may glean a love of geometry,
Poliphilus, Dominican monk,
could not see past a dream
of love outstruggling the Island,
place of love's desiring.

The outer rings of cypress and myrtle
manicured hedges encircling all species
of nimble lovers   yearning & flowering
     or lazing in the sun

ii   the dream garden's incarnation

Cat thyme and rue, lavender cotton
    and Southernwood.
Germander and marjoram. A green peacock
drinking from a bowl or buried deep in a bed
    of love-lies-bleeding.

Lilith and the Minotaur

i   vitriol

In the gown
of the seventh maiden

(Daedalus supplied the threads)

Lilith faced the Minotaur
confident that she
would be loved.

She warned of death
and said vitriol
would be his lament.

ii   splice

The Minotaur
drank Lilith's swelling heart
which would not be emptied

conscience spliced them together,
the Minotaur grew protective

the heart shrivelled,
and was emptied

iii   release

sympathy —
the mere thought
set her straight

she lured Theseus
to break this infatuation

she bled
a silver thread

Chimera Song

chimera calls the nightjar
sung double-faced in sun and shadow,
come together in old style on elder
ground expects Lilith to follow
    as it would itself

solicitous angels guard
their quarry well, not even chimera,
hidden at will, can nudge its way
through the bars and into her jail

chimera, watcher of the fluid Graces
take heart in what you gather —
the coldest whisper, the strainings
at Vespers, delight outbrooding
   a nightjar's flight

Aram Lily Songs

i

the confident centrepiece
quivers amongst the sheer
folds of its robes.

would you believe
death's mute obsession
speaks easy at night

or that bisque cupolas
turn into themselves
when placed indoors?

ii

the arrangement of lilies
on the sainfoin encrusted banks
is planned

      they do not open
wantonly, do not spill their seed
carelessly

iii

an old lady cuts lilies
in the early morning

her skin bubbles
under a red rash

she fills her basket
for the cemetery

these are the offspring of Lilith,
the lily is her flower

Lilith Considers Two Who
Have Died Young

Hart Crane

Keats had nothing on this one, he who hurled
and was hurled himself, he of the caustic waterfront
manner, singing songs by the wharves as the dead
drifted by. This one had a sweet tooth. And the ego was
there for the filling — I got to him once in a dentist's
chair and had him gloating over the prospect of genius,
of seventh heavens and seven spheres and wild dances
under the moon of aether, of arseholes on cold cell
floors, of suns rising and sinking beneath his feet,
of epic and graft, of a bottle of Mercurochrome
          that mapped a gut wrenching elegy.

Sylvia Plath

She offered her father
though in truth he wasn't
up to it. She offered her
lovers, even her husband.
I'd taken them a long
time back. The children,
strangely she refused.
Not to say she turned
me down flat, but rather
equivocated to a point
where the evaporating
flesh lost voice.

Lilith and Gunabibi Agree on Territory

Lilith: So, mine will be of darkness
and interminable cold; or of fire
and white heat. You can take
the temporal ground.

Gunabibi: I shall take the living. And I shall take
you should you choose a manifest life.
All are without time and dream the dream
I make them receptive to, though the dream
is not mine . . .

Lilith.   And I shall be God's messenger,
if you like.

Lilith Speaks

The pensive and subliminal
the conscience delicately
flexing its muscles
toning down love
discreetly

that offspring leap from bodies
chaste, when love is no more than
apparatus, appendage, decoration
to the mechanics . . .

                driven to an altered state
I slide into sweet non life,
always myself,
always part of the moist kiss
that numbs

A Note

Great evening thought Lilith —
they fed on my anecdotes,
drank my self effacements,
wiped their mouths
on my disasters . . .
Well I'll be damned
if I'll do their dishes.

A Brief Affair

She hated waking up next to him
stinking of booze he'd scream
'Get me a bucket I wanna
throw up!'
He'd spent half his life
in prison.
He drank whisky constantly now.
She had to
leave him — his hide was as tough
as concrete,
she couldn't break through.
For once, Lilith misjudged — when
she left he cried his eyes out.

Lilith and the Orange Tree

The young girl stood beside me. I
*   Saw not what her young eyes could see:*
— A light, she said, not of the sky
*   Lives somewhere in the Orange Tree.*
Shaw Neilson

Of course I was pulling his leg,
and didn't he lap it up — they all do,
I've pulled that trick a thousand times.

Not that some sort of light
doesn't appear, but this is always
after the fact — the poet recalling
a light was there, a light to accompany
his music of the spheres. Chills you
doesn't it? No, I don't feel bad — I never
do. In fact, I think I've brought a lot
of spiritual conviction to poetry
lovers over the years. And yes,
God does have a lot to thank me for.

Lilith Invites the Great Poet Czeslaw Milosz into Bosch's *Garden of Earthly Delights*

i

I am in the Prado watching the poet
watching the Garden of Earthly Delights.
I would like to know if he is seeking
to enter the painting or simply
view it. Already he is calling me Eve.

I lean out and arch behind him, looking over
his shoulder at what he is writing — 'So that I run to its waters
And immerse myself in them and recognise myself'.
So far so good. But what is this talk about centuries
closing, and bodily preservation, and senses outreaching
            themselves —
his share, like mine, is nothing. He's got a nice eye for
fashion, or the lack of, I'll admit. Though he's prone
to hallucination: there is no concept of Time in this painting.

ii

It was a ball because that was the shape of his shit.
Is nothing sacred?
                    Or maybe it was the ball Picasso's
acrobats threw into the field of the circus.
Though for this to have been the case the Prado
would need to have come to an agreement with the Stockholm
Gallery of Modern Art.

iii

This Paradise he's writing is not true
but so beautiful I could be fooled.
He says: 'This, then, is the Fountain
Of Life? Toothed, sharp-edged,
With its innocent, delusive colour. And beneath,
Just where the birds alight, glass traps set with glue'.
He apprehends the possibility of error
built into The Scheme of Things, too human
the mystery of the fruit is the Mother
of his doom. Can Time stretch
for those trapped in the rings of his wishes?
Let me tell him, the whole lot of them,
his incredible Form included, to walk on the filth
that is my bones, my prison. Had he been Adam,
had he been Eve, he would have felt
the same satisfaction in treading on me
as he did when he uncovered the Tree's duplicity.

iv

The naming of fish, fowl, and beast,
of nakedness and conjoining, of the rich liquid
that is sap that is the blood of the sun.
Pleasure denies its connotation. I have none of this,
though maybe my outstretched fingers tickle
his groin. No matter, the stars blind the night:
'Meanwhile a flock of lunar signs fills the sky
To prepare the alchemical nuptials of the planets'.

v

There's no getting away from it, the triptych
is a death that lives in the moment that refuses
to name itself. The abyss is large and comfortable
in its actions — like the evening which gathers
beneath floodlights, like curators calling Time.

The Three Faces of Lilith

i

The three faces of Lilith
revealed themselves in glances.
Above, the air softened,
                              softened
as the three faces struggled to look
into three different hearts.

ii

That behind these masks
the vegetative lurked,
                              soul vessel
shared threefold,
                              instantly recognisable,
instantly lost.

The hearts mimicked each other,
remaining unchanged, though taking
each feature as ornament.

iii

Inclination and Appetite,
Frailty and Honour and Shame,
they could not flatter
and remain sane — the most obvious
attempt fell flat, strained
their solicitous natures.

iv

Virtue — picking glass
          from the upholstery
          Lilith let it be known
          she had no time
          for little red convertibles,
          lear jets, or a seat
          at the Captain's table.

Three Hearts —
the First Revolution

i

The physical heart
could ward off danger
by virtue of its strength

Lilith of the physical heart
is confident, loud, enigmatic

Lilith of the physical heart
is lustful and easily
disappointed

ii

The bitter heart
consumes itself,
this
is Lilith
torn by isolation,
at her most dangerous,
her most vulnerable

iii

The growing heart
has an eye for itself
and will check its growth
if threatened — not that design
prevents Lilith, rather
the growing heart
knows its limits

Three Hearts — the Second Revolution

i

Lilith carries her fluid self
closer to change, keeping her back
to Gunabibi who flickers like a great snake
waiting for the sun to cloak its retreat.
The torn heart has lodged, the torn heart
has watered its blood down to the pink-orange
of cataclysm. The torn heart is dead.

ii

The spiritual heart has outgrown
itself, is looking to Heaven, has cast
indiscretion aside. As the eye reaches,
climbing espaliers of sight, it crosses
the verdigris of night and spreads.

ii

Full heart, blood on your copper wings,
full heart, in flight over the loveless waves,
full heart, hungering, fill yourself
with hope. Full heart, only patience
will bring Lilith back again.

Lilith's Pain

Aloof. Chest and shoulders
torn through — the three hearts
flown, flittering out like flies
from a blown carcass, though beautiful
in decay — the wings of Lilith
unfolding with her lifeblood.
And emerging from her moist cocoon,
Lilith left the trappings
of the telephone age to her old body,
and rose up out of the garden
in pursuit of the hearts.

Lilith and St Anthony

She barely touches the ground,
steps so lightly, swings her tresses
or tingles with cropped hair, she dances
so sweetly, and I love her for this,
I love her because she does not tempt me . . .
she is both fruitful and barren,
she inspires and empties,
her breath is dank and fresh
I love her for this . . .

Lilith Considers Two Others . . .

Rimbaud

To give him his due, he hated his name,
and he hated the way the scabs clustered about his
arsehole, the way governments and family
fucked him around. And he died young — in fact,
he died when he was about seven. When he noted
the colour of his mother's dresses, the texture
of his sister's undergarments, the grime
that gathered beneath his fingers. When he realised
that words were made up of letters, that letters
were devised to account for words. When he learnt
that the best poets were scatalogical; when he
made paper boats and set them loose on rivers;
when he considered the cost of clothing and arming
a soldier. When he called a name in his sleep.

Emily Dickinson

What's fifty-five years to the young at heart.
Ah, she was as supple as a six-year-old,
as sweet as a rose, as free as a butterfly.
It sounds too good to be true, doesn't it?
Well, look at it another way — she was as old
as Methuselah's mother, was old at the moment
of conception, looked me in the eye at birth
and strung together one of her weedy poems.
That she saved bits of string and wrapping paper
from Christmas, that she never got many poems
out because she begrudged paying for the postage.
So now, which version do you prefer? The one
in which her communion was with the trite,
the precious, or that with an eye to death.

Poems of Annunciation

i

the wand is as supple
as the wrist that winds
its charms

it is the strand of hair
the capillaries close to the surface,
the heart's form writ
over the page of her body

the wand is the pen
that signs off,
the signatory to arrivals
and departures

ii

the message never came out
the way it was intended,
the messenger put his or her
stamp on it, soothsaying
the truth out of language
into the realm of gesture

iii

Lilith sent herself
a message of hope

Lilith sent herself
a message of love

Lilith moved quickly
from the point of delivery
to the point of arrival

and of the hearts . . .

Cocoons

i

Gunabibi caught the hearts
and set them to spinning
cocoons — 'I'll see you
when you get out'
she said

ii

in their transitional sleep
the hearts reconciled differences,
and the dormant merged with the actual
and meshed itself against the prospect
of a new set of rules

iii

Gunabibi was surprised to see
the hearts had retained the capacity
of flight despite their long sleep

though she felt pleased with herself —
they were no longer part of Lilith,
who had long ago lost her grip on things

iv

the three faces
of one heart — steel-winged
            iron-beaked

                      spreading
from horizon to horizon,
                 exhaust rising
like the green dust
          of a burst puffball.

Beyond Durer's Nativity

The birds sit lightly, rafters slip
slowly back, stilled. Plantlife in rigid
pose abstains from growth. Enclosed
universe neat in its arch issues forth
its own angel in recognition.

An old man pours a libation of pure water.
Decay: clean and orderly. She, hands folded,
(Lilith was said to have lurked),
whispers in all tongues:
                              'il serait si doux l'aimer . . .'